T0022775

I always come away from reading Robert Murray McChenye feeling inspired, so it's a delight to have his writing distilled in this little book. *The Sweet Bond Christian Love* will stir your soul and renew your zeal for Jesus.

Tim Chester,
senior faculty member of Crosslands Training and
author of *Meeting Christ in the Garden*

We live in an age consumed by the trivial and superficial. Tragically, this has infected our thoughts about God and our understanding of our relationship with him. But this wonderful collection of material from Robert Murray McCheyne is like a clear breath of fresh air. McCheyne lived a brief life, but he knew the mighty God of the Bible. Because he knew God, he feared him, even as he communed with him. He was humbled, and he desired, above all, to serve the Savior faithfully. These excerpts point us in the same direction—to the mighty God who communes with his people by his Spirit to the glory of Jesus Christ.

Jonathan Master,
President, Greenville Presbyterian Theological Seminary;
author, *Reformed Theology*

The Sweet Bond of Christian Love

The Sweet Bond of Christian Love

A Collection of Quotes from

Robert Murray McCheyne

Copyright © Christian Focus Publications 2024

Hardback ISBN: 978-1-5271-1064-9
Ebook ISBN: 978-1-5271-1118-9

10 9 8 7 6 5 4 3 2 1

First published in 2024
in the Christian Heritage imprint
by
Christian Focus Publications Ltd,
Geanies House, Fearn, Ross-shire,
IV20 1TW, Great Britain

www.christianfocus.com

Cover by Rubner Durais

Typeset by Pete Barnsley (CreativeHoot.com)

Printed by Gutenberg, Malta

CONTENTS

INTRODUCTION

Robert Murray McCheyne was born in Edinburgh on 21 May 1813. In 1821, he enrolled in the Old High School, Edinburgh. From there, in November 1827, he went to the University of Edinburgh, and four years later, in November 1831, he commenced studies in the Divinity Hall. In 1832, McCheyne was assured of his salvation through reading *The Sum of Saving Knowledge*. He finished in the Divinity Hall in 1835 and was licensed to preach by the Presbytery of Annan. In November of that year, he became an assistant minister in Larbert and Dunipace. A year later, in November 1836, he became minister of St. Peter's Church of Scotland in Dundee.

In 1839, McCheyne had to take time away from St. Peter's because of heart problems. Later that year, he joined three ministers sent to assess the state of the Jews in Palestine and Europe (medical advice suggested the trip would help his health). He returned to Dundee in November, and began to participate in a revival which had commenced in his congregation and elsewhere during his absence under the ministry of W. C. Burns. In 1842, he devised his well-known Bible Reading Scheme initially for his congregation.

Sadly, McCheyne died of a fever on 25 March 1843. In December of that year, his close friend and ministerial colleague Andrew Bonar published the first edition of *The Memoir and Remains of the Reverend Robert Murray M'Cheyne*. Since then, it has been republished numerous times. Three years later, in 1846, *The Additional Remains of the late Rev. R. M. McCheyne* was also published.

This volume contains four sections. First, there is a biographical recollection of McCheyne composed by a friend, James Hamilton, who was a minister in London. Second, there is a collection of sayings by McCheyne. Third, there is a sermon by McCheyne on verses from the Song of Solomon, a biblical book from which McCheyne loved to preach. Fourth, there is his explanation of why he compiled his famous Daily Reading method.

RECOLLECTIONS OF
REV. ROBERT MURRAY McCHEYNE

JAMES HAMILTON[1]

Amongst Christian men a 'living epistle', and amongst Christian ministers, an 'able evangelist', is rare. Mr. M'Cheyne was both; and for the benefit of our readers, and to the praise of that grace which made him to differ, we would record a few particulars regarding one of whom we feel it no presumption to say that he was 'a disciple whom Jesus loved'.

God had given him a light and nimble form, which inclined him, in boyish days, for feats of agility, and enabled him in more important years to go through much fatigue, till the mainspring of the heart was

---

1   James Hamilton was born in 1814. His ministry began as assistant to Robert Smith Candlish at St. George's Church in Edinburgh (1838), after which he became an assistant minister in a parish in Perthshire (1839), which enabled his friendship with McCheyne and Andrew Bonar to increase. In July 1841, he became the minister of the National Scotch Church, Regent Square, London, where he would remain until his death in 1867. He wrote this article on 3 April 1843, shortly after McCheyne had passed away on 25 March.

weakened by overworking or disease. God had also given him a mind of which such a frame was the appropriate receptacle – active, expedite, full of enterprise, untiring and ingenious. He had a kind and quiet eye, which found out the living and beautiful in nature, rather than the majestic and sublime. Withal he had a pensive spirit which loved to muse on what he saw; and a lively fancy which scattered beauties of its own on what was already fair; and an idiom which expressed all his feelings exactly as he felt them, and gave simplicity and grace to the most common things he uttered. Besides, he had a delicate sensibility, a singularly tender manner, and an eminently affectionate heart. These are some of the gifts which he received at first from God, and which would have made him an interesting character though the grace of God had never given more.

He was born at Edinburgh twenty-nine years ago, and received his education at its High School and its College. When it was that the most important of all changes passed upon him, we do not know; but the change itself is described in some stanzas on 'Jehovah-Tsidkenu' which strikingly describe the difference between the emotions originating in a fine taste or tender feeling and those which spring from precious faith. At the two periods of its history his own susceptible mind had experienced either class.

He was only one-and-twenty when he became a preacher of the Gospel; and his first field of labour was Larbert, near Falkirk, where he was assistant minister about a year. That was the halcyon day of the Scotch Establishment before the civil power had laid its arrest on the energies of the Church and the hopes of the people. In every populous or neglected district new places of worship were springing up, with a rapidity which made grey-haired fathers weep for joy, thinking the glory of our second temple would surpass the glory of the first, and which promised in another generation to make Scotland a delightsome land again.

Among the rest a new church was built to the westward of Dundee – a district which combines almost everything desirable in a parish – not a few of the more intelligent and influential citizens in the near neighbourhood of its industrious artisans, whilst the flax-spinners of one locality are balanced by the almost rural population of another. The church was no sooner opened than it was fully occupied; and in selecting a minister, Mr. McCheyne was the choice of a unanimous congregation.

He entered on his labours in St. Peter's on November 27, 1836; and, as an earnest of coming usefulness, his first sermon was blessed to the salvation of some souls. When he became more minutely acquainted with his people, he found a few that feared the Lord and called upon his name; but the great mass of his congregation were mere churchgoers – under a form of godliness exhibiting little evidence of being new creatures in Christ; whilst he found throughout his parish such an amount of dissipation and irreverence and Sabbath-breaking, as plainly told that it was long since Willison had ceased from his labours.[2]

The state of his people pressed the spirit of this man of God, and put him on exertions which were not too great for the emergency, but which were far beyond his strength. He knew that nothing short of a living union to the second Adam could save from eternal death; and he also knew that nothing short of a new character would indicate this new relation. He was often in an agony till he should see Christ formed in the hearts of his people; and all the fertility of his mind was expended in efforts to present Christ and his righteousness in an aspect likely to arrest or allure them.

Like Moses, he spent much time in crying mightily to God in their behalf; and when he came out to meet them, the pathos of Jeremiah and the benignity of John were struggling in his bosom, and flitting over his transparent countenance by turns; and though he had much success, he had not all he wished, for he had not all his people. Many melted and were frozen up again; and many sat and listened to this ambassador

---

2   A reference to John Willison, a minister in Dundee in the previous century.

of Christ spending his vital energies in beseeching them, as if he himself were merely an interesting study, a phenomenon of earnestness. The vehemence of his desire and the intensity of his exertions destroyed his strength. It seemed as if the golden bowl were about to break; and, after two years' labour, a palpitation of the heart constrained him to desist.

Each step of a good man is ordered by the Lord. This 'step' – the sickness of Mr. McCheyne led to the visit of our Deputation to Palestine and gave a great impulse to that concern for Israel which is now a characteristic of Scottish Christianity; and the temporary loss of their pastor was the infinite gain of St. Peter's Church. When, after twelve months' separation, Mr. McCheyne returned, it was like a husbandman who has lain down lamenting that the heavens are brass and awakes amidst a plenteous rain. During his absence a singular outpouring of the Spirit had come down on his parish, and the ministry of his substitute was the means of a remarkable revival. Mr. M'Cheyne came back to find a great concern for salvation pervading his flock and many, whose carelessness had cost him bitter tears, 'cleaving to the Lord with full purpose of heart'.

We remember the Thursday evening when he first met his people again; the solemnity of his re-appearance in that pulpit, like one alive from the dead; his touching address, so true – 'And I, brethren, when I came to you, came not with excellency of speech';

and the overwhelming greeting which awaited him in the crowded street when the service was done – many, who had almost hated his ministry before, now pressing near to bless him in the name of the Lord.

From that time forward, with such discouragements as the impenitence of the ungodly, the inconsistency of doubtful professors, and the waywardness of real disciples occasionally caused him, his labours were wonderfully lightened. The presence of God was never wholly withdrawn; and besides some joyful communion-feasts, and several hallowed seasons of special prayer, almost every Sabbath brought its blessing. St. Peter's enjoyed a perennial awakening, a constant revival; and the effect was very manifest.

We do not say that the whole congregation or the whole parish shared it. Far from it. But an unusual number adorned the doctrine; and it was interesting on a Sabbath afternoon to see, as you passed along the street, so many of the working people keeping holy the Sabbath, often sitting, for the full benefit of the fading light, with their Bible or other book at the windows of their houses; and it was pleasant to think how many of these houses contained their pious inmates or praying families.

But it was in the church itself that you felt all the peculiarity of the place; and after being used to its heart-tuned melodies, its deep devotion, and solemn assemblies, and knowing how many souls had there been born to God, we own that we never came in sight of St. Peter's spire without feeling 'God is there'; and to this hour memory refuses to let go, wrapt round in heavenly associations, the well-known chime of its gathering bell, the joyful burst of its parting psalm, and, above all, that tender, pensive voice which was to many 'as though an angel spake to them'.

On Sabbath the 12th of March, he met his people for the last time. He felt weak, though his hearers were not aware of it. On the Tuesday following, some ministerial duty called him out; and, feeling very ill on his way home, he asked a friend to fulfil an engagement for him which he had undertaken for the subsequent day. He also begged his medical attendant to follow him home; and on reaching his house he set it in order, arranging his affairs, and then lay down on that bed from which he was never to arise. It was soon ascertained that, in visiting some people sick of the fever, he had caught the infection; and it was not long till the violence of the malady disturbed a mind unusually serene. At the outset of his trouble he seemed depressed and once begged to be left alone for half an hour. When the attendant returned he looked relieved and happy, and said with a smile, 'My soul is escaped as a bird out of the snare of a fowler'; and thenceforward, till his mind began to wander, he was in perfect peace.

During those last painful days of unconsciousness, he fancied he was engaged in his beloved work of preaching, and at other times prayed in a most touching manner, and at great length, for his people. His people were also praying for him; and on the evening of Friday se'nnight,[3] when it became known that his life was in danger, a weeping multitude assembled in St. Peter's, and with difficulty were dissuaded from continuing all night in supplication for him. Next morning he seemed a little revived, but it was only the gleam before the candle goes out. At a quarter-past nine he expired; and all that day nothing was to be heard in the houses around but lamentation and great mourning, and, as a friend in that neighbourhood writes, 'In passing along the high road you saw the faces of every one swollen with weeping.' On Thursday last, his hallowed remains were laid in St. Peter's burying-ground, their proper resting place till these heavens pass away.

If asked to mention the source of his abundant labours, as well as the secret of his holy, happy and successful life, we would answer, 'His faith was wonderful.' Being rationally convinced on all those points regarding which reason can form conclusions, and led by the Spirit into those assurances which lie beyond the attainment of mere reason, he surrendered himself fully to the power of these ascertained realities. The redemption which has already been achieved, and

---

3   An old word for seven days.

the glory which is yet to be unveiled, were as familiar to his daily convictions as the events of personal history; and he reposed with as undoubting confidence on the revealed love of the Father, Son and Spirit as ever he rested on the long tried affection of his dearest earthly kindred. With the simplicity of a little child he had received the kingdom of heaven; and, strengthened mightily by experience and the Spirit's indwelling, he held fast that which he had received.

A striking characteristic of his piety was absorbing love to the Lord Jesus. This was his ruling passion. It lightened all his labours, and made the reproaches which for Christ's sake sometimes fell on him, by identifying him more and more with his suffering Lord, unspeakably precious. He cared for no question unless his Master cared for it; and his main anxiety was to know the mind of Christ. He once told a friend, 'I bless God every morning I awake that I live in witnessing times.' And in a letter six months ago he says, 'I fear lest the enemy should so contrive his measures in Scotland as to divide the godly. May God make our way plain! It is comparatively easy to suffer when we see clearly that we are suffering members of Jesus.'

His public actings were a direct emanation from this most heavenly ingredient in his character – his love and gratitude to the Divine Redeemer. In this he much resembled one whose 'Letters' were almost daily his delight, Samuel Rutherford; and, like Rutherford, his adoring contemplations naturally gathered round them the imagery and language of the Song of Solomon. Indeed, he had preached so often on that beautiful book that at last he had scarcely left himself a single text of its 'good matter' which had not been discoursed on already.

It was very observable that, though his deepest and finest feelings clothed themselves in fitting words, with scarcely any effort, when he was descanting on the glory or grace of the Saviour, he despaired of transferring to other minds the emotions which were overfilling his own; and after describing those excellencies which often made the careless wistful, and made disciples marvel, he left the theme with evident regret that where he saw so much he could say so little. And so rapidly did he advance in scriptural and experimental acquaintance with Christ that it was like one friend learning more of the mind of another. And we doubt not that, when his hidden life is revealed, it will be found that his progressive holiness and usefulness coincided with those new aspects of endearment or majesty which, from time to time, he beheld in the face of Immanuel, just as the 'authority' of his 'gracious words', and the impressive sanctity of his demeanour, were so far a transference from him who spake as no man ever spake and lived as no man ever lived. In his case the words had palpable meaning, 'Beholding as in a glass the glory of the Lord, we are changed into the same image from glory to glory, as by the Spirit of the Lord.'

More than any one whom we have ever known, had he learned to do everything in the name of the Lord Jesus. Amidst all his humility, and it was very deep, he had a prevailing consciousness that he was one of those who belong to Christ; and it was from him, his living Head, that he sought strength for the discharge of duty, and through him, his righteousness, that he sought the acceptance of his performances. The effect was to impart habitual tranquillity and composure to his spirit. He committed his ways to the Lord and was sure that they would be brought to pass; and though his engagements were often numerous and pressing, he was enabled to go through them without hurry or perturbation. We can discern traces of this uniform self-possession in a matter so minute as his handwriting. His most rapid notes show no symptoms of haste or bustle, but end in the same neat and regular style in which they began; and this quietness of spirit accompanied him into the most arduous labours and critical emergencies. His effort was to do all in the Surety; and he proved that promise, 'Great peace have they which love thy law, and nothing shall offend them.'

He gave himself to prayer. Like his blessed Master, he often rose up a great while before it was day, and spent the time in prayer, and singing psalms and hymns, and the devotional reading of that Word which dwelt so richly in him. His walks, and rides, and journeys were sanctified by prayer. The last time he was leaving London we accompanied him to the railway station. He chose a place in an empty carriage, hoping to employ the day in his beloved exercise; but the arrival of other passengers invaded his retirement. There was nothing which he liked so much as to go out into a solitary place and pray; and the ruined chapel of Invergowrie, and many other sequestered spots around Dundee, were the much-loved resorts where he had often enjoyed sweet communion with God. Seldom have we known one so specific and yet reverential in his prayers, nor one whose confessions of sin united such self-loathing with such filial love. And now that 'Moses, my servant, is dead,' perhaps the heaviest loss to his brethren, his people, and the land is the loss of his intercessions.

He was continually about his Master's business. He used to seal his letters with a sun going down behind the mountains and the motto over it, 'The night cometh.' He felt that the time was short and studiously sought to deepen this impression on his mind. To solemnize his spirit for the Sabbath's services, he would visit some of his sick or dying hearers on the Saturday afternoon; for, as he himself once expressed it to the writer, 'Before preaching he liked to look over the verge.' Having in himself a monitor that his own sun would go early down, he worked while it was day; and, in his avidity to improve every opportunity, frequently brought on attacks of dangerous illness. The autumn after his return from Palestine many of his hearers were in an anxious state; and on the Sabbath before the labouring people amongst them set out for the harvest-work in the country, like Paul at Troas, he could not desist from addressing them and praying with them. In one way or other, from morning to midnight, with scarcely a moment's interval, he was exhorting, and warning, and comforting them; and the consequence was an attack of fever, which brought him very low.

But it was not only in preaching that he was thus faithful and importunate. He was instant in every season. In the houses of his people, and when he met them by the wayside, he would speak a kind and earnest word about their souls; and his words were like nails. They went in with such force that they usually fastened in a sure place. An instance came to our knowledge long ago. In the course of a ride one day, he was observing the operations of the workmen in a quarry; when passing the engine-house, he stopped for a moment to look at it. The engineman had just opened the furnace door to feed it with fresh fuel; when, gazing at the bright white glow within, Mr. McCheyne said to the man, in his own mild way, 'Does that fire mind you of anything?' And he said no more, but passed on his way. The man had been very careless, but could not get rid of this solemn question. To him it was the Spirit's arrow. He had no rest till he found his way to St. Peter's Church, where he became a constant attendant; and we would fain hope that he has now fled from the wrath to come.

His speech was seasoned with salt, and so were his letters. As was truly remarked in the discriminating and affectionate tribute to his memory, which recently appeared in the *Dundee Warder*, 'Every note from his hand had a lasting interest about it; for his mind was so full of Christ that, even in writing about the most ordinary affairs, he contrived, by some natural turn, to introduce the glorious subject that was always uppermost with him.' It was always quickening to hear from him. It was like climbing a hill, and, when weary or lagging, hearing the voice of a friend, who has got far up on the sunny heights, calling to you to arise and come away. The very subscriptions usually told where his treasure was: 'Grace be with you, as Samuel Rutherford would have prayed'; 'Ever yours till we meet above'; 'Ever yours till glory dawn, Robert M. McCheyne.'

The tenderness of his conscience, the truthfulness of his character, his deadness to the world, his deep humility and exalted devotion, his consuming love to Christ and the painful solicitude with which he eyed everything affecting his honour, the fidelity with which he denied himself and told others of their faults or danger, his meekness in bearing wrong, and his unwearied industry in doing good, the mildness which tempered his unyielding firmness and the jealousy for the Lord of Hosts which commanded, but did not supplant, the yearnings of a most affectionate heart rendered him altogether one of the loveliest specimens of the Spirit's workmanship. He is gone, and in his grave has been buried the sermon which, for the last six years, his mere presence has preached to Dundee. That countenance so kindly earnest, those gleams of holy joy flitting over its deeper lines of sadness, that disentangled pilgrim-look which showed plainly that he sought a city, the serene self-possession of one who walked by faith, and the sequestered musing gait such as we might suppose the meditative Isaac had, that aspect of compassion in such unison with the remonstrating and entreating tones of his melodious voice, that entire appearance as of one who had been with Jesus, and who would never be right at home till, where Christ is, there he should be also – all these come back on memory with a vividness which annihilates the interval since last we saw them, and with an air of immortality around them which promises that ere long we shall see them again.

To enjoy his friendship was a rare privilege in this world of defect and sin; and now that those blessed hours of personal intercourse are ended, we can recall many texts of which his daily walk was the easy interpretation. Any one may have a clearer conception of what is meant by a 'hidden life', and a 'living sacrifice', and may better understand the kind of life which Enoch led, who has lived a day with Robert Murray McCheyne.

SAYINGS
OF McCHEYNE

ADOPTION

O what a change for an heir of hell to become an heir of God, and joint heir with Christ, to inherit God, to have a son's interest in God! Eternity alone will teach you what is in that word, 'heir of God.'

When you were brought to believe on the Son of God, you were adopted into his family, fed with the children's bread, and your heart filled with the holy pleasures of God.

BIBLE CHARACTERS

Be like Barnabas, a son of consolation. The Lord humble, empty, satisfy, and fill you – make you a Boanerges and a Barnabas, all in one. Remember Barnabas' advice, 'Cleave to the Lord'; not to man, but to the Lord.

Pray to be made like Caleb, who had another spirit, and followed the Lord fully. Follow Christ all the day.

When Isaiah saw that God was so great a God, and so holy, he felt himself undone. He felt that he could not stand in the presence of so great a God. O brethren! have you ever had a discovery of the

highness and holiness of God, so as to lay you
low at his feet?

CHRISTIAN LIVING

Believers should live in daily consideration of the
greatness and glory of Christ.

Lift your eyes from your own bosom, downcast
believer; look upon Jesus. It is good to consider your
ways, but it is far better to consider Christ.

If the sheep is on the shoulder of the shepherd, it
is always getting nearer the fold. With some the
shepherd takes long steps.

You must be content then to lean all your
weight upon Christ.

The leaning soul cries for continued grace.

Live much in the smiles of God. Bask in his beams.
Feel his all-seeing eye settled on you in love, and
repose in his almighty arms.

It is one of the very beauties which Christ sees in his
people, that they are solitary among a world of thorns.

FAITH

Oh! what a wonderful thing the eye of faith is: it sees beyond the stars, it pierces to the throne of God, and there it looks on the face of Jesus making intercession for us, whom having not seen we love, in whom, though now we see him not, yet believing we rejoice with joy unspeakable and full of glory.

If you believe little, you will keep far off from Jesus.

UNCONVERTED

If an unconverted man were taken away into heaven, where Christ sits in glory, and if he overheard Christ's words of admiring love towards the believer, he could not understand them, he could not comprehend how Christ should see a loveliness in poor religious people whom he in the bottom of his heart despised.

Not only are Christless persons condemned already, but the instruments of their destruction are prepared and quite ready.

A natural man has not a spark of God's holiness in him…. You may be kind, pleasant, agreeable, good-natured, amiable people, there may be a kind of integrity about you, so that you are above stealing or lying; but as long as you are in a natural state, there is not a grain of God's holiness in you.

JUSTIFICATION

Because, justified in the eyes of Christ, washed in his blood, a believer is pure and white as a lily. Christ can see no spot in his own righteousness, and therefore he sees no spot on the believer.

I must not only wash in Christ's blood, but clothe me in Christ's obedience. For every sin of omission in self, I may find a divinely perfect obedience ready for me in Christ. For every sin of commission in self, I may find not only a stripe or a wound in Christ, but also a perfect rendering of the opposite obedience in my place, so that the law is magnified – its curse more than carried – its demand more than answered.

Believers differ in attainments, in gifts and graces, but all are equally justified before God.

DESIRE AND JESUS

The soul that is taught of God seeks for
a complete Saviour.

I ought to study Christ as a living Saviour more – as
a Shepherd, carrying the sheep he finds – as a King,
reigning in and over the souls he has redeemed – as
a Captain, fighting with those who fight with me,
Ps. 35 – as one who has engaged to bring me through
all temptations and trials, however impossible to
flesh and blood.

If we have been saved by Christ, we should pour
out our best affections on him. It is well to love his
disciples, well to love his ministers, well to love his
poor, but it is best to love himself.

If I know my own heart, its only desire is that Christ
may be glorified, by souls flocking to him, and abiding
in him, and reflecting his image; and whether it be in
Perth or Dundee, should signify little to us.

JOY

Some people are afraid of anything like joy in religion.
They have none themselves, and they do not love to

see it in others. Their religion is something like the stars, very high, and very clear, but very cold.

Believing in a manifested Christ fills the heart full of joy.

Believe none, and you will have no joy. Believe little, and you will have little joy. Believe much, and you will have much joy. Believe all, and you will have all joy, and your joy will be full.

No joy is like the Divine joy. It is infinite, full, eternal, pure, unmingled joy.

ELECTION

If Christ has visited your soul, give him all the glory. 'Not unto us, Lord, not unto us, but unto thy name give glory.' The only reason why you are saved is the sovereign compassion of Jesus.

'If I knew I were one of the elect I would come, but I fear I am not.' To you I answer: nobody ever came to Christ because they knew themselves to be of the elect. It is quite true that God has of his mere good pleasure elected some to everlasting life, but they never knew it till they came to Christ. Christ nowhere invites the elect to come to him. The question for you is not, 'Am I one of the elect?' but, 'Am I of the human race?'

He chose me from all eternity, else I never would have chosen him. He shed his blood for me, else I never would have shed a tear for him. He cried after me, else I never would have breathed after him. He sought after me, else I never would have sought after him. He hath loved me, therefore I love him. He hath chosen me, therefore I evermore choose him.

HEAVEN

Often on earth, when one believer begins to praise God for what he has done for his soul, it stirs up the hearts of others. So in heaven, when the angels hear the voice of redeemed sinners, brands plucked out of the fire, standing near the throne, they will obtain a ravishing view of the glory of God, his mercy and grace; they will fall down and worship God. They will not envy the redeemed their place; but on the contrary, be filled with intense praise by hearing of what God has done for their souls.

And if before he comes we should go away to be where he is, still we shall enter into a world of perpetual summer – we shall behold his glory which the Father gave him.

Ah! to all eternity the incarnation of Jesus will be the theme of our wonder and praise.

Go round every one in glory, every one has a different story, yet every one has a tale of suffering.

HOLY LIVING

A believer is to be known, not only by his peace and joy, but by his warfare and distress.

Remember it is God, and not man, that must have the glory.

Coming to Christ takes away your fear of the law, but it is the Holy Spirit coming into your heart that makes you love the law.

There is no argument like a holy life.

A living Christ is the spring of holiness to all his members.

Remember to take Christ home with you, and let him rule in your house. If you walk with Christ abroad but never take him home, you will soon part company for ever.

The love of Christ to man constraineth the believer to live a holy life, because that truth takes away all his dread and hatred of God.

You will get more holiness from immediate conversing with God than from all other means of grace put together. Indeed, the means are empty vanity, unless you come to God in them.

Communion with Christ is always sanctifying.

Oh! I wish that my heart were quite refined from all self-seeking. I am quite sure that our truest happiness is not to seek our own – just to forget ourselves and to fill up the little space that remains seeking only, and above all, that our God may be glorified.

I trust you feel real desire after complete holiness. This is the truest mark of being born again. It is a mark that he has made us meet for the inheritance of the saints in light.

Nothing stirs me up so much to be instant and faithful as hearing of the triumphs of the Lord Jesus in other places.

We must carry the cross, but only for a moment, then comes the crown.

Unfathomable oceans of grace are in Christ for you. Dive and dive again, you will never come to the bottom of these depths.

Do not take up your time so much with studying your own heart as with studying Christ's heart. For one look at yourself, take ten looks at Christ!

LIFE AND DEATH OF JESUS

The Gospels are the narrative of the heart of Jesus, of the work of Jesus, of the grace of Jesus.

In the manger at Bethlehem, there lay a perfect infant, but there also was Jehovah.

That mysterious being who rode on an ass's colt, and wept over Jerusalem, was as much a man as you are, and as much God as the Father is. The tears he shed were human tears, yet the love of Jehovah swelled below his mantle. That pale being that hung quivering on the cross was indeed man, it was human blood that flowed from his wounds, but he was as truly God.

What I wish you to observe, then, is, that it was an actual survey of the crowded cities, of the over-peopled villages, of the crowds that followed him; it was an actual sight and survey of these things, that moved the Saviour's compassion. His eye affected his heart.

Every member of his body and faculty of his mind were used only as servants to holiness. His mouth was the only human mouth from which none but gracious words ever proceeded. His eye was the only human eye that never shot forth flames of pride, or envy, or lust. His hand was the only human hand that never was stretched forth but in doing good. His heart was the only human heart that was not deceitful above all things and desperately wicked.

When Christ came and obeyed the law from the cradle to the grave, when the Son of God came and delighted to do the will of God, and had the law always in his heart, loving God with all his heart, and his neighbour as himself, this gave new lustre to the law. It showed to all worlds that it is the happiness and chief good of the creature to keep God's holy law.

'Father, I will.' This is the most wonderful prayer that ever rose from this earth to the throne of God, and this petition is the most wonderful in the prayer. No human lips ever prayed thus before.

Those few dark hours on Calvary, when the great high priest was offering up the amazing sacrifice, give light for eternity to the believing soul.

This only will cheer you in dying. Not your graces, nor your love to Christ; not anything in you, but only this, Christ hath died. He loved me, and gave himself for me.

The wounds of Christ were the greatest outlets of his glory that ever were.

LOVE

We shall spend eternity in loving God, in adoring, admiring, and praising God. We should spend much of our present time in this. Some people imagine that they are not serving God unless they are visiting the sick, or engaged in some outward service; whereas the highest of all service is the love of adoration in the soul.

Love God for ever and ever because he chose you of his own free will. Adore Jesus, that he passed by millions, and died for you. Adore the Holy Ghost, that he came out of free sovereign mercy and awakened you.

When we are brought to see the reconciled face of God in peace, that is a great privilege. But how can we look upon that face, reconciling and reconciled, and not love him who hath so loved us! Love begets love.

Soon we shall exchange the table below for the table above, where we shall give full expression to our love to all eternity.

MEDITATION AND COMMUNION

When we become Christians, we become acquainted with the persons of the Godhead.

I ought to spend the best hours of the day in communion with God. It is my noblest and most fruitful employment, and is not to be thrust into any corner. The morning hours, from six to eight, are the most uninterrupted, and should be thus employed, if I can prevent drowsiness.

Paul got such a view of the glory, brightness, and excellency of the way of salvation by Jesus that it filled his whole heart.

A look from the eye of Christ to Peter broke and melted his proud heart; he went out and wept bitterly. Pray that a single look of that broken bread may do the same for you.

Does the cross of Christ fill your heart? Does it make a great calm in your soul, a heavenly rest?

Do you sit within sight of the cross? Does your soul rest there?

Sit down like Mary, and gaze upon a crucified Jesus. So will the world become a dim and dying thing. When you gaze upon the sun, it makes everything else dark; when you taste honey, it makes everything else tasteless; so when your soul feeds on Jesus, it takes away the sweetness of all earthly things.

He that hath seen a weeping Christ hath seen the Father.

There is greater rest and solace to be found in the presence of God for one hour than in an eternity of the presence of man.

There is no book of the Bible which affords a better test of the depth of a man's Christianity than the Song of Solomon.

Live within sight of Calvary, and you will live within sight of glory.

MEETING WITH JESUS

Christ's coming to the desolate believer is often sudden and wonderful.

His eye rests on the houses of this town, where his jewels live. Christ loves some streets far better than others – some spots of earth are far dearer to him than others.

The Lord Jesus cannot bear that we should have a nearer friend than himself. He must be our next of kin.

Christ is not done with a soul when he has brought it to the forgiveness of sins. It is only then that he begins his regular visits to the soul. In the daily reading of the Word, Christ pays daily visits to sanctify the believing soul. In daily prayer, Christ reveals himself to his own in that other way than he doth to the world.

It is the presence of Christ that makes a sweet time of refreshing in a church.

The closer we walk with Christ now, the closer will we walk with him to all eternity.

The believer is unspeakably precious in the eyes of Christ, and Christ is unspeakably precious in the eyes of the believer.

To you that know Jesus, and his grace. Oh! study him more. You will spend eternity in beholding his glory; spend time in beholding his grace.

There is enough in Jesus to keep thy soul. The ocean is full of drops, but Christ's bosom is more full of grace.

PASTORING

So it is said of the angels that 'they do always behold the face of my Father which is in heaven'. Even when most engaged in the service of the saints, they feel under his all-seeing, holy, living eye. So ought faithful ministers to feel. They should feel constantly in his presence, under his soul-piercing, gentle-guiding, holy, living eye.

The faithful minister should feel the presence of a living Saviour.

In great measure, according to the purity and perfections of the instrument, will be the success. It is not great talents God blesses so much as great likeness to Jesus. A holy minister is an awful weapon in the hand of God.

I am persuaded that I shall obtain the highest amount of present happiness, I shall do most for God's glory and the good of man, and I shall have the fullest reward in eternity, by maintaining a conscience always washed in Christ's blood, by being filled with the Holy Spirit at all times, and by attaining the most entire likeness to Christ in mind, will, and heart, that it is possible for a redeemed sinner to attain to in this world.

Ah! dear friend, wherever we journey, union to Jesus and holiness from his Spirit flowing into us, is our chief and only happiness. Never cease to show your people that to be holy is to be happy; and that, to bring us to perfect holiness and likeness to God, was the very end for which Christ died.

O for a pastor who unites the deep knowledge of [Jonathan] Edwards, the vast statements of [John] Owen, and the vehement appeals of Richard Baxter!

Do not rest without success in your ministry. Success is the rule under a living ministry; want of success is the exception.

He that puts the treasure into earthen vessels, often allows the vessels to be chipped and broken, that the excellency of the power may be of God and not of us.

As I was walking in the fields, the thought came over me with almost overwhelming power, that every one of my flock must soon be in heaven or hell. O how I wished that I had a tongue like thunder, that I might make all hear; or that I had a frame like iron, that I might visit every one, and say, 'Escape for thy life! Ah, sinners! you little know how I fear that you will lay the blame of your damnation at my door.'

PRAYER

The corn in harvest sometimes ripens more in one day than in weeks before. So some Christians gain more grace in one day than for months before. Pray that this may be a ripening harvest day in your souls.

Most Christians have need to cast their formal prayers away, to be taught to cry, Abba.
I was preaching in Perth last Sabbath; when I came out, a little girl came up to me, I think about three or four years old. She wanted to hear of the way to be saved. Her mother said she had been crying the whole night before about her soul, and would take no comfort till she should find Jesus.

Abraham was the friend of God, and got very near to God in prayer, but he prayed as dust and ashes. 'I have taken upon me to speak unto God that am but dust and ashes.' Jacob had power with God, and prevailed, yet his boldest word was, 'I will not let thee go except thou bless me.' Daniel was a man greatly beloved, and got immediate answers to prayer, and yet he cried to God as a sinner – 'O Lord, hear! O Lord, forgive! O Lord, hearken and do!' Paul was a man who got very near to God, and yet he says, 'I bow my knees to the God and Father of our Lord Jesus Christ.' But when Christ prayed, he cried, 'Father, I will.'

There never was, and never will be, a believing prayer
left unanswered.

No person can be a child of God without living in
secret prayer; and no community of Christians can be
in a lively condition without unity in prayer.

Rose early to seek God, and found him whom
my soul loveth. Who would not rise early to
meet such company?

Awoke early by the kind providence of God, and
had uncommon freedom and fervency in keeping the
concert for prayer this morning before light.

PREACHING

'I determined to know nothing among you, but Jesus
Christ and him crucified.' This was the beginning,
and middle, and end of the preaching of Paul.

It is a glorious thing to preach the unsearchable
riches of Christ.

The grand work of the minister, in which he is to
lay out his strength of body and mind, is preaching.

Weak and foolish as it may appear, this is the grand instrument which God has put into our hands, by which sinners are to be saved, and saints fitted for glory.

It is not the work of the minister to open up schemes of human wisdom or learning, nor to bring his own fancies, but to tell the acts and glories of the Gospel. We must speak of what is within the Word of God.

This is the reason why many good men have a barren ministry. They speak from clear head-knowledge, or from past experience, but not from a present grasp of the truth, not from a present sight of the Lamb of God. Hence their words fall like a shower of snow, fair and beautiful, but cold and freezing.

O brethren, it is thus only we can ever speak with feeling, or with power, or with truth, of the unsearchable riches of Christ. We must have the taste of the manna in our mouth, 'Milk and honey under our tongue,' else we cannot tell of its sweetness. We must be drinking the living water from the smitten rock, or we cannot speak of its refreshing power. We must be hiding our guilty souls in the wounds of Jesus, or we cannot with joy speak of the peace and rest to be found there.

It is the testimony of an old divine, who was indeed a master in Israel, 'That the main benefit obtained by preaching is, by impression made upon the mind at the time, and not by remembering what was delivered.'

When he sits under the preached word, and hears the voice of the Shepherd leading and feeding his soul, it reminds him of the day when the Lamb that is in the midst of the throne shall feed him and lead him to living fountains of waters.

Some good men cry, Flee, flee, without showing the sinner what he is to flee from; and again, they cry, Come, come, without showing plainly the way of pardon and peace. These men act as one would do who should run through the streets crying, Fire, fire, without telling where.

SIN AND BACKSLIDING

You fear that your convictions of sin have not been deep enough. This is no reason for keeping away from Christ. You will never get a truly broken heart till you are really in Christ.

Ah! children of God, it is a fearful sign to see little thirst in you. I do not wonder much when the world stay away from our meetings for the Word and prayer; but, ah! when you do, I am dumb, my soul will weep in secret places for your pride.

There is nothing more distressing in our day than the want of growth among the children of God. They do not seem to press forward; they do not seem to be running a race.

I must never think a sin too small to need immediate application to the blood of Christ.

None but God knows what an abyss of corruption is in my heart. He knows and covers all in the blood of the Lamb.

Think, my beloved friends, that every act of unholiness, of conformity to the world, of selfishness, of whispering and backbiting, is hindering the work of God in the parish, and ruining souls eternally.

Even those that are most deeply concerned about their souls do not see the millionth part of the blackness of their hearts and lives.

SORROW AND SUFFERING

Every one that gets to the throne must put their foot
upon the thorn. The way to the crown is by the cross.
We must taste the gall if we are to taste the glory.

The way to Zion is through the valley of Baca. You
must go through the wilderness of Jordan if you are
to come to the Land of Promise.

Some believers are much surprised when they are
called to suffer. They thought they would do some
great thing for God; but all that God permits them to
do is to suffer.

Perhaps God gets more glory by a single adoring look
of some poor believer on a sick bed than from the
outward labours of a whole day.

It is one of the laws of Christ's kingdom, 'We must
through much tribulation enter into the kingdom of
God.' We must not reckon upon a smooth road to
glory, but it will be a short one.

TEMPTATIONS

Ah! believers, you are a tempted people. You are always poor and needy. And God intends it should be so, to give you constant errands to go to Jesus.

Believers complain of Satan, but they never felt his power as Christ did.

Are you sore tempted in soul, put into trying circumstances, so that you know not what to do? Look up; he is able to succour you. If he had been on the earth would you not have gone to him? Would you not have kneeled and said, 'Lord, help me?' Does it make any difference that he is at the right hand of God? He is the same yesterday, today, and for ever.

SALVATION

Have you not lived long enough in pleasure? Come and try the pleasures of Christ – forgiveness and a new heart. I have not been at a dance or any worldly amusement for many years, and yet I believe I have had more pleasure in a single day than you have had all your life. In what? you will say. In feeling that God loves me, that Christ has washed me and in feeling that I shall be in heaven when the wicked are cast into hell.

The first conviction that is essential to the conversion of the soul is conviction of sin; not the general conviction that all men are sinful, but the personal conviction that I am an undone sinner; not the general conviction that other men must be forgiven or perish, but the personal conviction that I must be forgiven or perish.

The way to be saved is to know God's heart and the heart of Jesus.

All your peace is to be found in believing God's Word about his Son.

Christ is the bush that has been burned yet not consumed. Oh! it is a safe place for a hell-deserving sinner to rest.

THE WORK OF THE SPIRIT

Jesus has obtained the gift of the Holy Spirit as a reward of his work. It is fitting that he that died

for sinners should have the Spirit to dispense
to whom he will.

Let your soul be filled with a heart-ravishing sense
of the sweetness and excellency of Christ and all that
is in Him. Let the Holy Spirit fill every chamber of
your heart; and so there will be no room for folly, or
the world, or Satan, or the flesh.

Keep your eye upon Jesus and the unsearchable riches
that are in him; and may the gentle Comforter fill
your soul, and give you a sweet foretaste of the glory
that is to follow.

THE LORD'S DAY

The Lord's Day is his property. Just as the Lord's
Supper is the supper belonging to Christ. It is his
table. He is the bread. He is the wine. He invites
the guests. He fills them with joy and with the Holy
Ghost. So it is with the Lord's Day. All days of the
year are Christ's, but he hath marked out one in seven
as peculiarly his own.

And we love the Lord's Day, because it is his. Every
hour of it is dear to us – sweeter than honey, more
precious than gold. It is the day he rose for our

justification. It reminds us of his love, and his finished work, and his rest.

Spend the Lord's Day in the Lord's presence. Spend it as a day in heaven. Spend much of it in praise and in works of mercy, as Jesus did.

SERMON

(PREACHED IN 1837)

> 'As the lily among thorns, so is my love among the
> daughters. As the apple-tree among the trees of the
> wood, so is my beloved among the sons. I sat down
> under his shadow with great delight, and his fruit
> was sweet unto my taste' (Song of Solomon 2:2, 3).

If an unconverted man were taken away into heaven,
where Christ sits in glory, and if he overheard Christ's
words of admiring love towards the believer, he could
not understand them, he could not comprehend how
Christ should see a loveliness in poor religious people
whom he in the bottom of his heart despised. Or again,
if an unconverted man were to overhear a Christian at
his devotions when he is really within the veil, and were
to listen to his words of admiring, adoring love towards
Christ, he could not possibly understand them, he
could not comprehend how the believer should have
such a burning affection towards one unseen, in whom

he himself saw no form nor comeliness. So true it is that the natural man knoweth not the things of the Spirit of God, for they are foolishness unto him.

There may be some now hearing me who have a rooted dislike to religious people, they are so stiff, so precise, so gloomy, you cannot endure their company. Well then, see here what Christ thinks of them, 'As the lily among thorns, so is my love among the daughters.' How different you are from Christ! There may be some hearing me who have no desires after Jesus Christ, who never think of him with pleasure; you see no form nor comeliness in him, no beauty that you should desire him; you do not love the melody of his name; you do not pray to him continually. Well then, see here what the believer thinks of him, how different from you: 'As the apple-tree among the trees of the wood, so is my beloved among the sons. I sat down under his shadow with great delight, and his fruit was sweet to my taste.' O that you would be awakened by this very thing, that you are so different from Christ, and so different from the believer, to think that you must be in a natural condition, you must be under wrath!

Doctrine. The believer is unspeakably precious in the eyes of Christ, and Christ is unspeakably precious in the eyes of the believer.

1. INQUIRE WHAT CHRIST THINKS OF THE BELIEVER.

'As the lily among the thorns, so is my love among the daughters.' Christ sees nothing so fair in all this world as the believer. All the rest of the world is like thorns, but the believer is like a beautiful lily in his eyes. When you are walking in a wilderness all overgrown with briers and thorns, if your eye falls upon some lonely flower, tall and white, and pure and graceful, growing in the midst of the thorns, it looks peculiarly beautiful. If it were in the midst of some rich garden among many other flowers, then it would not be so remarkable; but when it is encompassed with thorns on every side, then it engages the eye. Such is the believer in the eyes of Christ. 'As the lily among thorns, so is my love among the daughters.'

(1) See what Christ thinks of the unconverted world. It is like a field full of briers and thorns in his eyes.

(a) Because fruitless. 'Do men gather grapes of thorns, or figs of thistles?' So Christ gets no fruit from the unconverted world. It is all one wide, thorny waste.

(b) Because, when the word is preached among them, it is like sowing among thorns. 'Break up your fallow ground and sow not among thorns.' When the sower sowed, some fell among thorns, and the thorns sprang up and choked them; so is preaching to the unconverted.

(c) Because their end will be like that of thorns; they are dry and fit only for the burning. 'As thorns cut up shall they be burned in the fire.' 'For the earth, which is often rained upon and only bears thorns and briers, is rejected, and nigh unto cursing, whose end is to be burned.' My friends, if you are not in a Christian state, see what you are in the eyes of Christ – thorns. You think that you have many admirable qualities, that you are valuable members of society, and you have a hope that it shall be well with you in eternity. See what Christ says — you are thorns and briers, useless in this world, and fit only for the burning.

(2) See what Christ thinks of the believer. 'As the lily among thorns so is my love among the daughters.' The believer is like a lovely flower in the eyes of Christ.

(a) Because, justified in the eyes of Christ, washed in his blood, he is pure and white as a lily. Christ can see no spot in his own righteousness, and therefore he sees no spot on the believer. 'Thou art all fair, my love, as a lily among thorns so is my love.'

(b) a believer's nature is changed. Once he was like the barren, prickly thorn, fit only for burning; now Christ has put a new spirit in him; the dew has been given to him, and he grows up like the lily. Christ loves the new creature. 'All my delight is in them.' 'As the lily among thorns so is my love among the daughters.' Are you a Christian? Then never mind though the world despise you, though they call you names; remember Christ loves you, he calls you 'my love.' Abide in him, and you shall abide in his love. 'If ye continue in my word, then are ye my disciples indeed.'

(c) Because so lonely in the world. Observe, there is but one lily, but many thorns. There is a great wilderness all full of thorns, and only one lonely flower. So there is a world lying in wickedness, and a little flock that believe in Jesus. Some believers are cast down because they feel solitary and alone. If I be in the right way, surely I would not be so lonely. Surely the wise, and the amiable, and the kind people I see round about me, surely, if there were any truth in religion, they would know it. Be not cast down. It is one of the marks of Christ's people that they are alone in the world, and yet they are not alone. It is one of the very beauties which Christ sees in his people, that they are solitary among a world of thorns. 'As a lily among thorns, so is my love among the daughters.'

Do not be discouraged. This world is the world of loneliness. When you are transplanted to yon garden of God, then you shall be no more lonely, then you shall be away from all the thorns. As flowers in a rich garden blend together their thousand odours to enrich the passing breeze, so, in the paradise above, you shall join the thousands of the redeemed blending with theirs the odour of your praise. You shall join with the redeemed as living flowers to form a garland for the Redeemer's brow.

2. INQUIRE WHAT THE BELIEVER THINKS OF CHRIST.

'As the apple-tree among the trees of the wood, so is my beloved among the sons. I sat down under his shadow with great delight, and his fruit was sweet to my taste.'

(1) Christ is more precious than all other saviours in the eye of the believer. As a traveller prefers an apple-tree to every other tree of the wood because he finds both shelter and nourishing food under it, so the believer prefers Christ to all other saviours. When a man is travelling in eastern countries, he is often like to drop down under the burning rays of the sun. It is a great relief when he comes to a wood. When Israel were travelling in the wilderness, they came to Elim, where were twelve wells of water, and seventy palm-trees, and they encamped there by the water. They were glad of the shelter of the trees. So Micah says that God's people 'dwell solitarily in the wood'; and Ezekiel promises, 'they shall sleep in the woods.' But if the traveller be hungry and faint for lack of food, then he will not be content with any tree of the wood, but he will choose out a fruit tree, under which he may sit down and find nourishment as well as shade. He sees a fair apple-tree – he chooses it out of all the trees of

the wood, because he can both sit under its shadow and eat its pleasant fruits.

So is it with the soul awakened by God. He feels under the heat of God's anger; he is in a weary land; he is brought into the wilderness; he is like to perish; he comes to a wood; many trees offer their shade; where shall he sit down? Under the fir-tree? Alas! what fruit has it to give? He may die there. Under the cedar tree, with its mighty branches? Alas! he may perish there; for it has no fruit to give. The soul that is taught of God seeks for a complete Saviour. The apple-tree is revealed to the soul. The hungry soul chooses that evermore. He needs to be saved from hell and nourished for heaven. 'As the apple-tree among the trees of the wood, so is my beloved among the sons.'

Awakened souls, remember you must not sit down under every tree that offers itself. Take heed that no one deceive you; for many shall come in Christ's name, saying, I am Christ, and deceive many. There are many ways of saying peace, peace, when there is no peace. You will be tempted to find peace in the world, in self-repentance, in self-reformation. Remember, choose you a tree that will yield fruit as well as shade. 'As the apple-tree among the trees of the wood, so is my beloved among the sons. Pray for a choosing faith. Pray for an eye to discern the apple-tree. Oh! there is no rest for the soul except under that Branch which

God has made strong. My heart's desire and prayer for you is, that you may all find rest there.

(2) Why has the believer so high an esteem of Christ?

Answer 1. Because he has made trial of Christ. 'I sat down under his shadow with great delight.' All true believers have sat down under the shadow of Christ. Some people think that they shall be saved because they have got a head-knowledge of Christ. They read of Christ in the Bible, they hear of Christ in the house of God, and they think that is to be a Christian. Alas! my friends, what good would you get from an apple-tree, if I were only to describe it to you; tell you how beautiful it was, how heavily laden with delicious apples? Or, if I were only to show you a picture of the tree, or if I were to show you the tree itself at a distance, what the better would you be? You would not get the good of its shade or its pleasant fruit. Just so, dear brethren, what good will you get from Christ, if you only hear of him in books and sermons, or if you see him pictured forth in the sacrament, or if you were to see him with your bodily eye? What good would all this do if you do not sit down under his shadow? O my friends, there must be a personal sitting down under the shadow of Christ, if you would be saved. Christ is the bush that has been burned yet not consumed. Oh! it is a safe place for a hell-deserving sinner to rest.

Some may be hearing me who can say, 'I sat down under his shadow.' And yet you have forsaken him. Ah! have you gone after your lovers, and away from Christ? Well, then, may God hedge up your way with thorns. Return, return, O Shulamite! There is no other refuge for your soul. Come and sit down again under the shadow of the Saviour.

Answer 2. Because he sat down with great delight. (1) Some people think there is no joy in religion, it is a gloomy thing. When a young person becomes a Christian, they would say, Alas! he must bid farewell to pleasure, farewell to the joys of youth, farewell to a merry heart. He must exchange these pleasures for reading of the Bible and dry sermon-books, for a life of gravity and preciseness. This is what the world says. What does the Bible say? 'I sat down under his shadow with great delight.' Ah! let God be true, and every man a liar. Yet no one can believe this except those who have tried it. Ah! be not deceived, my young friends; the world has many sensual and many sinful delights; the delights of eating and drinking, and wearing gay clothes; the delights of revelry and the dance. No man of wisdom will deny that these things are delightful to the natural heart; but oh! they perish in the using, and they end in an eternal hell. But to sit down under the shadow of Christ, wearied with God's burning anger, wearied with seeking after vain saviours, at last to find rest under the shadow of Christ, ah! this is great delight. Lord, evermore may I sit under this shadow! Lord, evermore may I filled with this joy!

(2) Some people are afraid of anything like joy in religion. They have none themselves, and they do not love to see it in others. Their religion is something like the stars, very high, and very clear, but very cold. When they see tears of anxiety, or tears of joy, they cry out, Enthusiasm, enthusiasm! Well, then, to the Law and to the Testimony. 'I sat down under his shadow with great delight.' Is this enthusiasm? O Lord, evermore give us this enthusiasm! May the God of hope fill you with all joy and peace in believing! If it be really in sitting under the shadow of Christ, let there be no bounds to your joy. O if God would but open your eyes, and give you simple, child-like faith to look to Jesus, to sit under his shadow, then would songs of joy rise from all our dwellings. Rejoice in the Lord always, and again, I say, rejoice!

(3) Because the fruit of Christ is sweet to the taste. All true believers not only sit under the shadow, but partake of his pleasant fruits; just as when you sit under an apple-tree, the fruit hangs above you and around you, and invites you to put out the hand and taste; so, when you come to submit to the righteousness of God, and bow your head, and sit down under Christ's shadow, all other things are added unto you.

First, temporal mercies are sweet to the taste. None but those of you who are Christians know this, when you sit under the shadow of Christ's temporal mercies, because covenant mercies. 'Bread shall be given you; your water shall be sure.' These are sweet apples from the tree, Christ. O Christian, tell me, is not bread sweeter when eaten thus? Is not water richer than wine? And Daniel's pulse better than the dainties of the King's table?

Second, afflictions are sweet to the taste. Every good apple has some sourness in it. So it is with the apples of the tree, Christ. He gives afflictions as well as mercies. He sets the teeth on edge; but even these are blessings in disguise – they are covenant gifts. Oh! affliction is a dismal thing when you are not under his shadow. But are you Christians? Look on your sorrows as apples from that blessed tree. If you knew how wholesome they are, you would not wish to lack them. Several of you know it is no contradiction to say, these apples, though sour, are sweet to my taste.

Third, the gifts of the Spirit are sweet to the taste. Ah! here is the best fruit that grows on the tree: here are the ripest apples from the topmost branch. You who are Christians know how often your soul is fainting. Well, here is nourishment to your fainting soul. Everything you need is in Christ. 'My grace is sufficient for thee.' Dear Christian, sit much under that tree – feed much upon that fruit. 'Stay me with flagons, comfort me with apples, for I am sick of love.'

Fourth, promises of glory. Some of the apples have a taste of heaven in them. Feed upon these, dear Christians. Some of Christ's apples give you a relish for the fruit of Canaan – for the clusters of Eshcol. Lord, evermore give me these apples; for oh! they are sweet to my taste.

DAILY BREAD,

BEING A CALENDAR FOR READING THROUGH THE WORD OF GOD IN A YEAR

'Thy Word is very pure; therefore thy servant loveth it.'

My Dear Flock,

The approach of another year stirs up within me new desires for your salvation, and for the growth of those of you who are saved. 'God is my record how greatly I long after you all in the bowels of Jesus Christ.' What the coming year is to bring forth who can tell? There is plainly a weight lying on the spirits of all good men, and a looking for some strange work of judgment coming upon this land. There is need now to ask that solemn question, 'If in the land of peace wherein thou trustedst, they wearied thee, then how wilt thou do in the swelling of Jordan?

Those believers will stand firmest who have no dependence upon self or upon creatures, but upon

Jehovah our Righteousness. We must be driven more to our Bibles, and to the mercy seat, if we are to stand in the evil day. Then we shall be able to say like David, 'The proud have had me greatly in derision, yet have I not declined from thy law.' 'Princes have persecuted me without a cause, but my heart standeth in awe of thy Word.'

It has long been in my mind to prepare a scheme of Scripture reading, in which as many as were made willing by God might agree, so that the whole Bible might be read once by you in the year, and all might be feeding in the same portion of the green pasture at the same time. I am quite aware that such a plan is accompanied with many *dangers*.

1. *Formality*. We are such weak creatures that any regularly returning duty is apt to degenerate into a lifeless form. The tendency of reading the Word by a fixed rule may, in some minds, be to create this skeleton religion. This is to be the peculiar sin of the last days: 'Having the form of godliness, but denying the power thereof.' Guard against this. Let the calendar perish rather than this rust eat up your souls.

2. *Self-righteousness*. Some, when they have devoted their set time to reading the Word, and accomplished their prescribed portion, may be tempted to look at themselves with self-complacency. Many, I am persuaded, are living without any Divine work on their soul – unpardoned, and unsanctified, and ready

to perish – who spend their appointed times in secret and family devotion. This is going to hell with a lie in the right hand.

3. *Careless reading.* Few tremble at the Word of God. Few, in reading it, hear the voice of Jehovah, which is full of majesty. Some, by having so large a portion, may be tempted to weary of it, as Israel did of the daily manna, saying— "Our soul loatheth this light bread; "and to read it in a slight and careless manner. This would be fearfully provoking to God. Take heed lest that word be true of you- 'Ye said, also, Behold, what a weariness is it! and ye have snuffed at it, saith the Lord of Hosts."

4. *A yoke too heavy to bear.* Some may engage in reading with alacrity for a time, and afterwards feel it a burden grievous to be borne. They may find conscience dragging them through the appointed task without any relish of the heavenly food. If this be the case with any, throw aside the fetter and feed at liberty in the sweet garden of God. My desire is not to cast a snare upon you, but to be a helper of your joy.

If there be so many dangers, why propose such a scheme at all? To this I answer, that the best things are accompanied with danger, as the fairest flowers are often gathered in the clefts of some dangerous precipice. Let us weigh *the advantages.*

1. *The whole Bible will be read through in an orderly manner in the course of a year* – the Old Testament

once, the New Testament and Psalms twice. I fear many of you never read the whole Bible; and yet it is all equally Divine: 'All Scripture is given by inspiration of God, and is profitable for doctrine, for reproof, for correction, and instruction in righteousness, that the man of God may be perfect.' If we pass over some parts of Scripture, we shall be incomplete Christians.

2. *Time will not be wasted in choosing what portions to read.* Often believers are at a loss to determine towards which part of the mountains of spices they should bend their steps. Here the question will be solved at once in a very simple manner.

3. *Parents will have a regular subject upon which to examine their children and servants.* It is much to be desired that family worship were made more instructive than it generally is. The mere reading of the chapter is often too like water spilt on the ground. Let it be read by every member of the family beforehand, and then the meaning and application drawn out by simple question and answer. The calendar will be helpful in this. Friends, also, when they meet, will have a subject for profitable conversation in the portions read that day. The meaning of difficult passages may be inquired from the more judicious and ripe Christians, and the fragrance of simpler Scriptures spread abroad.

4. *The pastor will know in what part of the pasture the flock are feeding.* He will thus be enabled to speak more suitably to them on the Sabbath; and both pastor and

elders will be able to drop a word of light and comfort in visiting from house to house, which will be more readily responded to.

5. *The sweet bond of Christian love and unity will be strengthened.* We shall be often led to think of those dear brothers and sisters in the Lord, here and elsewhere, who agree to join with us in reading these portions. We shall oftener be led to agree on earth, touching something we shall ask of God. We shall pray over the same promises, mourn over the same confessions, praise God in the same songs, and be nourished by the same words of eternal life.

DIRECTIONS

1. The first column contains the day of the month. The next two columns contain the chapter to be read in the family. The two last columns contain the portions to be read in secret.

2. The head of the family should previously read over the chapter for family worship, and mark two or three of the most prominent verses, upon which he may dwell, asking a few simple questions.

3. Frequently the chapter named in the calendar for family reading might be read more suitably in secret; in which case the head of the family should intimate that it be read in private, and the chapter for secret reading may be used in the family.

4. The metrical version of the Psalms should be read or sung through at least once in the year. It is truly an admirable translation from the Hebrew, and is frequently more correct than the prose version. If three verses be sung at each diet of family worship, the whole Psalms will be sung through in the year.

5. Let the conversation at family meals often turn upon the chapter read and the psalm sung. Thus every meal will be a Sacrament, being sanctified by the Word and prayer.

6. Let our secret reading prevent the dawning of the day. Let God's voice be the first we hear in the morning. Mark two or three of the richest verses, and pray over every line and word of them. Let the marks be neatly done, never so as to abuse a copy of the Bible.

7. In meeting believers on the street or elsewhere, when an easy opportunity offers, recur to the chapters read that morning. This will be a blessed exchange for those idle words which waste the soul and grieve the Holy Spirit of God. In writing letters to those at a distance, make use of the provision that day gathered.

8. Above all, use the word as a lamp to your feet and a light to your path – your guide in perplexity – your armour in temptation – your food in times of faintness. Hear the constant cry of the great Intercessor, 'Sanctify them through thy truth. Thy word is truth.'

DATE	FAMILY		SECRET	
Jan. 1	Gen. 1	Matt. 1	Ezra 1	Acts 1
Jan. 2	Gen. 2	Matt. 2	Ezra 2	Acts 2
Jan. 3	Gen. 3	Matt. 3	Ezra 3	Acts 3
Jan. 4	Gen. 4	Matt. 4	Ezra 4	Acts 4
Jan. 5	Gen. 5	Matt. 5	Ezra 5	Acts 5
Jan. 6	Gen. 6	Matt. 6	Ezra 6	Acts 6
Jan. 7	Gen. 7	Matt. 7	Ezra 7	Acts 7
Jan. 8	Gen. 8	Matt. 8	Ezra 8	Acts 8
Jan. 9	Gen. 9–10	Matt. 9	Ezra 9	Acts 9
Jan. 10	Gen. 11	Matt. 10	Ezra 10	Acts 10
Jan. 11	Gen. 12	Matt. 11	Neh. 1	Acts 11
Jan. 12	Gen. 13	Matt. 12	Neh. 2	Acts 12
Jan. 13	Gen. 14	Matt. 13	Neh. 3	Acts 13
Jan. 14	Gen. 15	Matt. 14	Neh. 4	Acts 14
Jan. 15	Gen. 16	Matt. 15	Neh. 5	Acts 15
Jan. 16	Gen. 17	Matt. 16	Neh. 6	Acts 16
Jan. 17	Gen. 18	Matt. 17	Neh. 7	Acts 17
Jan. 18	Gen. 19	Matt. 18	Neh. 8	Acts 18
Jan. 19	Gen. 20	Matt. 19	Neh. 9	Acts 19
Jan. 20	Gen. 21	Matt. 20	Neh. 10	Acts 20
Jan. 21	Gen. 22	Matt. 21	Neh. 11	Acts 21
Jan. 22	Gen. 23	Matt. 22	Neh. 12	Acts 22
Jan. 23	Gen. 24	Matt. 23	Neh. 13	Acts 23
Jan. 24	Gen. 25	Matt. 24	Esther 1	Acts 24
Jan. 25	Gen. 26	Matt. 25	Est. 2	Acts 25
Jan. 26	Gen. 27	Matt. 26	Est. 3	Acts 26
Jan. 27	Gen. 28	Matt. 27	Est. 4	Acts 27

DATE	FAMILY		SECRET	
Jan. 28	Gen. 29	Matt. 28	Est. 5	Acts 28
Jan. 29	Gen. 30	Mark 1	Est. 6	Rom. 1
Jan. 30	Gen. 31	Mark 2	Est. 7	Rom. 2
Jan. 31	Gen. 32	Mark 3	Est. 8	Rom. 3
Feb. 1	Gen. 33	Mark 4	Est. 9–10	Rom. 4
Feb. 2	Gen. 34	Mark 5	Job 1	Rom. 5
Feb. 3	Gen. 35–36	Mark 6	Job 2	Rom. 6
Feb. 4	Gen. 37	Mark 7	Job 3	Rom. 7
Feb. 5	Gen. 38	Mark 8	Job 4	Rom. 8
Feb. 6	Gen. 39	Mark 9	Job 5	Rom. 9
Feb. 7	Gen. 40	Mark 10	Job 6	Rom. 10
Feb. 8	Gen. 41	Mark 11	Job 7	Rom. 11
Feb. 9	Gen. 42	Mark 12	Job 8	Rom. 12
Feb. 10	Gen. 43	Mark 13	Job 9	Rom. 13
Feb. 11	Gen. 44	Mark 14	Job 10	Rom. 14
Feb. 12	Gen. 45	Mark 15	Job 11	Rom. 15
Feb. 13	Gen. 46	Mark 16	Job 12	Rom. 16
Feb. 14	Gen. 47	Luke 1:1–38	Job 13	1 Cor. 1
Feb. 15	Gen. 48	Luke 1:39–80	Job 14	1 Cor. 2
Feb. 16	Gen. 49	Luke 2	Job 15	1 Cor. 3
Feb. 17	Gen. 50	Luke 3	Job 16–17	1 Cor. 4
Feb. 18	Ex. 1	Luke 4	Job 18	1 Cor. 5
Feb. 19	Ex. 2	Luke 5	Job 19	1 Cor. 6
Feb. 20	Ex. 3	Luke 6	Job 20	1 Cor. 7
Feb. 21	Ex. 4	Luke 7	Job 21	1 Cor. 8
Feb. 22	Ex. 5	Luke 8	Job 22	1 Cor. 9
Feb. 23	Ex. 6	Luke 9	Job 23	1 Cor. 10

DATE	FAMILY		SECRET	
Feb. 24	Ex. 7	Luke 10	Job 24	1 Cor. 11
Feb. 25	Ex. 8	Luke 11	Job 25–26	1 Cor. 12
Feb. 26	Ex. 9	Luke 12	Job 27	1 Cor. 13
Feb. 27	Ex. 10	Luke 13	Job 28	1 Cor. 14
Feb. 28	Ex. 11:1–12:21	Luke 14	Job 29	1 Cor. 15
Mar. 1	Ex. 12:22–51	Luke 15	Job 30	1 Cor. 16
Mar. 2	Ex. 13	Luke 16	Job 31	2 Cor. 1
Mar. 3	Ex. 14	Luke 17	Job 32	2 Cor. 2
Mar. 4	Ex. 15	Luke 18	Job 33	2 Cor. 3
Mar. 5	Ex. 16	Luke 19	Job 34	2 Cor. 4
Mar. 6	Ex. 17	Luke 20	Job 35	2 Cor. 5
Mar. 7	Ex. 18	Luke 21	Job 36	2 Cor. 6
Mar. 8	Ex. 19	Luke 22	Job 37	2 Cor. 7
Mar. 9	Ex. 20	Luke 23	Job 38	2 Cor. 8
Mar. 10	Ex. 21	Luke 24	Job 39	2 Cor. 9
Mar. 11	Ex. 22	John 1	Job 40	2 Cor. 10
Mar. 12	Ex. 23	John 2	Job 41	2 Cor. 11
Mar. 13	Ex. 24	John 3	Job 42	2 Cor. 12
Mar. 14	Ex. 25	John 4	Prov. 1	2 Cor. 13
Mar. 15	Ex. 26	John 5	Prov. 2	Gal. 1
Mar. 16	Ex. 27	John 6	Prov. 3	Gal. 2
Mar. 17	Ex. 28	John 7	Prov. 4	Gal. 3
Mar. 18	Ex. 29	John 8	Prov. 5	Gal. 4
Mar. 19	Ex. 30	John 9	Prov. 6	Gal. 5
Mar. 20	Ex. 31	John 10	Prov. 7	Gal. 6
Mar. 21	Ex. 32	John 11	Prov. 8	Eph. 1
Mar. 22	Ex. 33	John 12	Prov. 9	Eph. 2

DATE	FAMILY		SECRET	
Mar. 23	Ex. 34	John 13	Prov. 10	Eph. 3
Mar. 24	Ex. 35	John 14	Prov. 11	Eph. 4
Mar. 25	Ex. 36	John 15	Prov. 12	Eph. 5
Mar. 26	Ex. 37	John 16	Prov. 13	Eph. 6
Mar. 27	Ex. 38	John 17	Prov. 14	Phil. 1
Mar. 28	Ex. 39	John 18	Prov. 15	Phil. 2
Mar. 29	Ex. 40	John 19	Prov. 16	Phil. 3
Mar. 30	Lev. 1	John 20	Prov. 17	Phil. 4
Mar. 31	Lev. 2–3	John 21	Prov. 18	Col. 1
Apr. 1	Lev. 4	Ps. 1–2	Prov. 19	Col. 2
Apr. 2	Lev. 5	Ps. 3–4	Prov. 20	Col. 3
Apr. 3	Lev. 6	Ps. 5–6	Prov. 21	Col. 4
Apr. 4	Lev. 7	Ps. 7–8	Prov. 22	1 Thess. 1
Apr. 5	Lev. 8	Ps. 9	Prov. 23	1 Thess. 2
Apr. 6	Lev. 9	Ps. 10	Prov. 24	1 Thess. 3
Apr. 7	Lev. 10	Ps. 11–12	Prov. 25	1 Thess. 4
Apr. 8	Lev. 11–12	Ps. 13–14	Prov. 26	1 Thess. 5
Apr. 9	Lev. 13	Ps. 15–16	Prov. 27	2 Thess. 1
Apr. 10	Lev. 14	Ps. 17	Prov. 28	2 Thess. 2
Apr. 11	Lev. 15	Ps. 18	Prov. 29	2 Thess. 3
Apr. 12	Lev. 16	Ps. 19	Prov. 30	1 Tim. 1
Apr. 13	Lev. 17	Ps. 20–21	Prov. 31	1 Tim. 2
Apr. 14	Lev. 18	Ps. 22	Eccles. 1	1 Tim. 3
Apr. 15	Lev. 19	Ps. 23–24	Eccles. 2	1 Tim. 4
Apr. 16	Lev. 20	Ps. 25	Eccles. 3	1 Tim. 5
Apr. 17	Lev. 21	Ps. 26–27	Eccles. 4	1 Tim. 6
Apr. 18	Lev. 22	Ps. 28–29	Eccles. 5	2 Tim. 1

DATE	FAMILY		SECRET	
Apr. 19	Lev. 23	Ps. 30	Eccles. 6	2 Tim. 2
Apr. 20	Lev. 24	Ps. 31	Eccles. 7	2 Tim. 3
Apr. 21	Lev. 25	Ps. 32	Eccles. 8	2 Tim. 4
Apr. 22	Lev. 26	Ps. 33	Eccles. 9	Titus 1
Apr. 23	Lev. 27	Ps. 34	Eccles. 10	Titus 2
Apr. 24	Num. 1	Ps. 35	Eccles. 11	Titus 3
Apr. 25	Num. 2	Ps. 36	Eccles. 12	Philem. 1
Apr. 26	Num. 3	Ps. 37	Song 1	Heb. 1
Apr. 27	Num. 4	Ps. 38	Song 2	Heb. 2
Apr. 28	Num. 5	Ps. 39	Song 3	Heb. 3
Apr. 29	Num. 6	Ps. 40–41	Song 4	Heb. 4
Apr. 30	Num. 7	Ps. 42–43	Song 5	Heb. 5
May 1	Num. 8	Ps. 44	Song 6	Heb. 6
May 2	Num. 9	Ps. 45	Song 7	Heb. 7
May 3	Num. 10	Ps. 46–47	Song 8	Heb. 8
May 4	Num. 11	Ps. 48	Isa. 1	Heb. 9
May 5	Num. 12–13	Ps. 49	Isa. 2	Heb. 10
May 6	Num. 14	Ps. 50	Isa. 3–4	Heb. 11
May 7	Num. 15	Ps. 51	Isa. 5	Heb. 12
May 8	Num. 16	Ps. 52–54	Isa. 6	Heb. 13
May 9	Num. 17–18	Ps. 55	Isa. 7	James 1
May 10	Num. 19	Ps. 56–57	Isa. 8:1–9:7	James 2
May 11	Num. 20	Ps. 58–59	Isa. 9:8–10:4	James 3
May 12	Num. 21	Ps. 60–61	Isa. 10:5–34	James 4
May 13	Num. 22	Ps. 62–63	Isa. 11–12	James 5
May 14	Num. 23	Ps. 64–65	Isa. 13	1 Pet. 1
May 15	Num. 24	Ps. 66–67	Isa. 14	1 Pet. 2

DATE	FAMILY		SECRET	
May 16	Num. 25	Ps. 68	Isa. 15	1 Pet. 3
May 17	Num. 26	Ps. 69	Isa. 16	1 Pet. 4
May 18	Num. 27	Ps. 70–71	Isa. 17–18	1 Pet. 5
May 19	Num. 28	Ps. 72	Isa. 19–20	2 Pet. 1
May 20	Num. 29	Ps. 73	Isa. 21	2 Pet. 2
May 21	Num. 30	Ps. 74	Isa. 22	2 Pet. 3
May 22	Num. 31	Ps. 75–76	Isa. 23	1 John 1
May 23	Num. 32	Ps. 77	Isa. 24	1 John 2
May 24	Num. 33	Ps. 78:1–37	Isa. 25	1 John 3
May 25	Num. 34	Ps. 78:38–72	Isa. 26	1 John 4
May 26	Num. 35	Ps. 79	Isa. 27	1 John 5
May 27	Num. 36	Ps. 80	Isa. 28	2 John 1
May 28	Deut. 1	Ps. 81–82	Isa. 29	3 John 1
May 29	Deut. 2	Ps. 83–84	Isa. 30	Jude 1
May 30	Deut. 3	Ps. 85	Isa. 31	Rev. 1
May 31	Deut. 4	Ps. 86–87	Isa. 32	Rev. 2
June 1	Deut. 5	Ps. 88	Isa. 33	Rev. 3
June 2	Deut. 6	Ps. 89	Isa. 34	Rev. 4
June 3	Deut. 7	Ps. 90	Isa. 35	Rev. 5
June 4	Deut. 8	Ps. 91	Isa. 36	Rev. 6
June 5	Deut. 9	Ps. 92–93	Isa. 37	Rev. 7
June 6	Deut. 10	Ps. 94	Isa. 38	Rev. 8
June 7	Deut. 11	Ps. 95–96	Isa. 39	Rev. 9
June 8	Deut. 12	Ps. 97–98	Isa. 40	Rev. 10
June 9	Deut. 13–14	Ps. 99–101	Isa. 41	Rev. 11
June 10	Deut. 15	Ps. 102	Isa. 42	Rev. 12
June 11	Deut. 16	Ps. 103	Isa. 43	Rev. 13

DATE	FAMILY		SECRET	
June 12	Deut. 17	Ps. 104	Isa. 44	Rev. 14
June 13	Deut. 18	Ps. 105	Isa. 45	Rev. 15
June 14	Deut. 19	Ps. 106	Isa. 46	Rev. 16
June 15	Deut. 20	Ps. 107	Isa. 47	Rev. 17
June 16	Deut. 21	Ps. 108–109	Isa. 48	Rev. 18
June 17	Deut. 22	Ps. 110–111	Isa. 49	Rev. 19
June 18	Deut. 23	Ps. 112–113	Isa. 50	Rev. 20
June 19	Deut. 24	Ps. 114–115	Isa. 51	Rev. 21
June 20	Deut. 25	Ps. 116	Isa. 52	Rev. 22
June 21	Deut. 26	Ps. 117–118	Isa. 53	Matt. 1
June 22	Deut. 27:1-28:19	Ps. 119:1–24	Isa. 54	Matt. 2
June 23	Deut. 28:20-68	Ps. 119:25–48	Isa. 55	Matt. 3
June 24	Deut. 29	Ps. 119:49–72	Isa. 56	Matt. 4
June 25	Deut. 30	Ps. 119:73–96	Isa. 57	Matt. 5
June 26	Deut. 31	Ps. 119:97–120	Isa. 58	Matt. 6
June 27	Deut. 32	Ps. 119:121–144	Isa. 59	Matt. 7
June 28	Deut. 33–34	Ps. 119:145-176	Isa. 60	Matt. 8
June 29	Josh. 1	Ps. 120–122	Isa. 61	Matt. 9
June 30	Josh. 2	Ps. 123–125	Isa. 62	Matt. 10
July 1	Josh. 3	Ps. 126–128	Isa. 63	Matt. 11
July 2	Josh. 4	Ps. 129–131	Isa. 64	Matt. 12
July 3	Josh. 5:1–6:5	Ps. 132–134	Isa. 65	Matt. 13
July 4	Josh. 6:6–27	Ps. 135–136	Isa. 66	Matt. 14
July 5	Josh. 7	Ps. 137–138	Jer. 1	Matt. 15
July 6	Josh. 8	Ps. 139	Jer. 2	Matt. 16
July 7	Josh. 9	Ps. 140–141	Jer. 3	Matt. 17
July 8	Josh. 10	Ps. 142–143	Jer. 4	Matt. 18

DATE	FAMILY		SECRET	
July 9	Josh. 11	Ps. 144	Jer. 5	Matt. 19
July 10	Josh. 12–13	Ps. 145	Jer. 6	Matt. 20
July 11	Josh. 14–15	Ps. 146–147	Jer. 7	Matt. 21
July 12	Josh. 16–17	Ps. 148	Jer. 8	Matt. 22
July 13	Josh. 18–19	Ps. 149–150	Jer. 9	Matt. 23
July 14	Josh. 20–21	Acts 1	Jer. 10	Matt. 24
July 15	Josh. 22	Acts 2	Jer. 11	Matt. 25
July 16	Josh. 23	Acts 3	Jer. 12	Matt. 26
July 17	Josh. 24	Acts 4	Jer. 13	Matt. 27
July 18	Judg. 1	Acts 5	Jer. 14	Matt. 28
July 19	Judg. 2	Acts 6	Jer. 15	Mark 1
July 20	Judg. 3	Acts 7	Jer. 16	Mark 2
July 21	Judg. 4	Acts 8	Jer. 17	Mark 3
July 22	Judg. 5	Acts 9	Jer. 18	Mark 4
July 23	Judg. 6	Acts 10	Jer. 19	Mark 5
July 24	Judg. 7	Acts 11	Jer. 20	Mark 6
July 25	Judg. 8	Acts 12	Jer. 21	Mark 7
July 26	Judg. 9	Acts 13	Jer. 22	Mark 8
July 27	Judg. 10:1–11:11	Acts 14	Jer. 23	Mark 9
July 28	Judg. 11:12–40	Acts 15	Jer. 24	Mark 10
July 29	Judg. 12	Acts 16	Jer. 25	Mark 11
July 30	Judg. 13	Acts 17	Jer. 26	Mark 12
July 31	Judg. 14	Acts 18	Jer. 27	Mark 13
Aug. 1	Judg. 15	Acts 19	Jer. 28	Mark 14
Aug. 2	Judg. 16	Acts 20	Jer. 29	Mark 15
Aug. 3	Judg. 17	Acts 21	Jer. 30–31	Mark 16
Aug. 4	Judg. 18	Acts 22	Jer. 32	Ps. 1–2

DATE	FAMILY		SECRET	
Aug. 5	Judg. 19	Acts 23	Jer. 33	Ps. 3–4
Aug. 6	Judg. 20	Acts 24	Jer. 34	Ps. 5–6
Aug. 7	Judg. 21	Acts 25	Jer. 35	Ps. 7–8
Aug. 8	Ruth 1	Acts 26	Jer. 36	Ps. 9
Aug. 9	Ruth 2	Acts 27	Jer. 37	Ps. 10
Aug. 10	Ruth 3–4	Acts 28	Jer. 38	Ps. 11–12
Aug. 11	1 Sam. 1	Rom. 1	Jer. 39	Ps. 13–14
Aug. 12	1 Sam. 2	Rom. 2	Jer. 40	Ps. 15–16
Aug. 13	1 Sam. 3	Rom. 3	Jer. 41	Ps. 17
Aug. 14	1 Sam. 4	Rom. 4	Jer. 42	Ps. 18
Aug. 15	1 Sam. 5–6	Rom. 5	Jer. 43	Ps. 19
Aug. 16	1 Sam. 7–8	Rom. 6	Jer. 44	Ps. 20–21
Aug. 17	1 Sam. 9	Rom. 7	Jer. 46	Ps. 22
Aug. 18	1 Sam. 10	Rom. 8	Jer. 47	Ps. 23–24
Aug. 19	1 Sam. 11	Rom. 9	Jer. 48	Ps. 25
Aug. 20	1 Sam. 12	Rom. 10	Jer. 49	Ps. 26–27
Aug. 21	1 Sam. 13	Rom. 11	Jer. 50	Ps. 28–29
Aug. 22	1 Sam. 14	Rom. 12	Jer. 51	Ps. 30
Aug. 23	1 Sam. 15	Rom. 13	Jer. 52	Ps. 31
Aug. 24	1 Sam. 16	Rom. 14	Lam. 1	Ps. 32
Aug. 25	1 Sam. 17	Rom. 15	Lam. 2	Ps. 33
Aug. 26	1 Sam. 18	Rom. 16	Lam. 3	Ps. 34
Aug. 27	1 Sam. 19	1 Cor. 1	Lam. 4	Ps. 35
Aug. 28	1 Sam. 20	1 Cor. 2	Lam. 5	Ps. 36
Aug. 29	1 Sam. 21–22	1 Cor. 3	Ezek. 1	Ps. 37
Aug. 30	1 Sam. 23	1 Cor. 4	Ezek. 2	Ps. 38
Aug. 31	1 Sam. 24	1 Cor. 5	Ezek. 3	Ps. 39

DATE	FAMILY		SECRET	
Sept. 1	1 Sam. 25	1 Cor. 6	Ezek. 4	Ps. 40–41
Sept. 2	1 Sam. 26	1 Cor. 7	Ezek. 5	Ps. 42–43
Sept. 3	1 Sam. 27	1 Cor. 8	Ezek. 6	Ps. 44
Sept. 4	1 Sam. 28	1 Cor. 9	Ezek. 7	Ps. 45
Sept. 5	1 Sam. 29–30	1 Cor. 10	Ezek. 8	Ps. 46–47
Sept. 6	1 Sam. 31	1 Cor. 11	Ezek. 9	Ps. 48
Sept. 7	2 Sam. 1	1 Cor. 12	Ezek. 10	Ps. 49
Sept. 8	2 Sam. 2	1 Cor. 13	Ezek. 11	Ps. 50
Sept. 9	2 Sam. 3	1 Cor. 14	Ezek. 12	Ps. 51
Sept. 10	2 Sam. 4–5	1 Cor. 15	Ezek. 13	Ps. 52–54
Sept. 11	2 Sam. 6	1 Cor. 16	Ezek. 14	Ps. 55
Sept. 12	2 Sam. 7	2 Cor. 1	Ezek. 15	Ps. 56–57
Sept. 13	2 Sam. 8–9	2 Cor. 2	Ezek. 16	Ps. 58–59
Sept. 14	2 Sam. 10	2 Cor. 3	Ezek. 17	Ps. 60–61
Sept. 15	2 Sam. 11	2 Cor. 4	Ezek. 18	Ps. 62–63
Sept. 16	2 Sam. 12	2 Cor. 5	Ezek. 19	Ps. 64–65
Sept. 17	2 Sam. 13	2 Cor. 6	Ezek. 20	Ps. 66–67
Sept. 18	2 Sam. 14	2 Cor. 7	Ezek. 21	Ps. 68
Sept. 19	2 Sam. 15	2 Cor. 8	Ezek. 22	Ps. 69
Sept. 20	2 Sam. 16	2 Cor. 9	Ezek. 23	Ps. 70–71
Sept. 21	2 Sam. 17	2 Cor. 10	Ezek. 24	Ps. 72
Sept. 22	2 Sam. 18	2 Cor. 11	Ezek. 25	Ps. 73
Sept. 23	2 Sam. 19	2 Cor. 12	Ezek. 26	Ps. 74
Sept. 24	2 Sam. 20	2 Cor. 13	Ezek. 27	Ps. 75–76
Sept. 25	2 Sam. 21	Gal. 1	Ezek. 28	Ps. 77
Sept. 26	2 Sam. 22	Gal. 2	Ezek. 29	Ps. 78:1–37
Sept. 27	2 Sam. 23	Gal. 3	Ezek. 30	Ps. 78:38–72

DATE	FAMILY		SECRET	
Sept. 28	2 Sam. 24	Gal. 4	Ezek. 31	Ps. 79
Sept. 29	1 Kings 1	Gal. 5	Ezek. 32	Ps. 80
Sept. 30	1 Kings 2	Gal. 6	Ezek. 33	Ps. 81–82
Oct. 1	1 Kings 3	Eph. 1	Ezek. 34	Ps. 83–84
Oct. 2	1 Kings 4–5	Eph. 2	Ezek. 35	Ps. 85
Oct. 3	1 Kings 6	Eph. 3	Ezek. 36	Ps. 86
Oct. 4	1 Kings 7	Eph. 4	Ezek. 37	Ps. 87–88
Oct. 5	1 Kings 8	Eph. 5	Ezek. 38	Ps. 89
Oct. 6	1 Kings 9	Eph. 6	Ezek. 39	Ps. 90
Oct. 7	1 Kings 10	Phil. 1	Ezek. 40	Ps. 91
Oct. 8	1 Kings 11	Phil. 2	Ezek. 41	Ps. 92–93
Oct. 9	1 Kings 12	Phil. 3	Ezek. 42	Ps. 94
Oct. 10	1 Kings 13	Phil. 4	Ezek. 43	Ps. 95–96
Oct. 11	1 Kings 14	Col. 1	Ezek. 44	Ps. 97–98
Oct. 12	1 Kings 15	Col. 2	Ezek. 45	Ps. 99–101
Oct. 13	1 Kings 16	Col. 3	Ezek. 46	Ps. 102
Oct. 14	1 Kings 17	Col. 4	Ezek. 47	Ps. 103
Oct. 15	1 Kings 18	1 Thess. 1	Ezek. 48	Ps. 104
Oct. 16	1 Kings 19	1 Thess. 2	Dan. 1	Ps. 105
Oct. 17	1 Kings 20	1 Thess. 3	Dan. 2	Ps. 106
Oct. 18	1 Kings 21	1 Thess. 4	Dan. 3	Ps. 107
Oct. 19	1 Kings 22	1 Thess. 5	Dan. 4	Ps. 108–109
Oct. 20	2 Kings 1	2 Thess. 1	Dan. 5	Ps. 110–111
Oct. 21	2 Kings 2	2 Thess. 2	Dan. 6	Ps. 112–113
Oct. 22	2 Kings 3	2 Thess. 3	Dan. 7	Ps. 114–115
Oct. 23	2 Kings 4	1 Tim. 1	Dan. 8	Ps. 116
Oct. 24	2 Kings 5	1 Tim. 2	Dan. 9	Ps. 117–118

DATE	FAMILY		SECRET	
Oct. 25	2 Kings 6	1 Tim. 3	Dan. 10	Ps. 119:1–24
Oct. 26	2 Kings 7	1 Tim. 4	Dan. 11	Ps. 119:25–48
Oct. 27	2 Kings 8	1 Tim. 5	Dan. 12	Ps. 119:49–72
Oct. 28	2 Kings 9	1 Tim. 6	Hosea 1	Ps. 119:73–96
Oct. 29	2 Kings 10	2 Tim. 1	Hos. 2	Ps. 119:97–120
Oct. 30	2 Kings 11–12	2 Tim. 2	Hos. 3–4	Ps. 119:121–144
Oct. 31	2 Kings 13	2 Tim. 3	Hos. 5–6	Ps. 119:145–176
Nov. 1	2 Kings 14	2 Tim. 4	Hos. 7	Ps. 120–122
Nov. 2	2 Kings 15	Titus 1	Hos. 8	Ps. 123–125
Nov. 3	2 Kings 16	Titus 2	Hos. 9	Ps. 126–128
Nov. 4	2 Kings 17	Titus 3	Hos. 10	Ps. 129–131
Nov. 5	2 Kings 18	Philem. 1	Hos. 11	Ps. 132–134
Nov. 6	2 Kings 19	Heb. 1	Hos. 12	Ps. 135–136
Nov. 7	2 Kings 20	Heb. 2	Hos. 13	Ps. 137–138
Nov. 8	2 Kings 21	Heb. 3	Hos. 14	Ps. 139
Nov. 9	2 Kings 22	Heb. 4	Joel 1	Ps. 140–141
Nov. 10	2 Kings 23	Heb. 5	Joel 2	Ps. 142
Nov. 11	2 Kings 24	Heb. 6	Joel 3	Ps. 143
Nov. 12	2 Kings 25	Heb. 7	Amos 1	Ps. 144
Nov. 13	1 Chron. 1–2	Heb. 8	Amos 2	Ps. 145
Nov. 14	1 Chron. 3–4	Heb. 9	Amos 3	Ps. 146–147
Nov. 15	1 Chron. 5–6	Heb. 10	Amos 4	Ps. 148–150
Nov. 16	1 Chron. 7–8	Heb. 11	Amos 5	Luke 1:1–38
Nov. 17	1 Chron. 9–10	Heb. 12	Amos 6	Luke 1:39–80
Nov. 18	1 Chron. 11–12	Heb. 13	Amos 7	Luke 2
Nov. 19	1 Chron. 13–14	James 1	Amos 8	Luke 3
Nov. 20	1 Chron. 15	James 2	Amos 9	Luke 4

DATE	FAMILY		SECRET	
Nov. 21	1 Chron. 16	James 3	Obad. 1	Luke 5
Nov. 22	1 Chron. 17	James 4	Jonah 1	Luke 6
Nov. 23	1 Chron. 18	James 5	Jonah 2	Luke 7
Nov. 24	1 Chron. 19–20	1 Pet. 1	Jonah 3	Luke 8
Nov. 25	1 Chron. 21	1 Pet. 2	Jonah 4	Luke 9
Nov. 26	1 Chron. 22	1 Pet. 3	Micah 1	Luke 10
Nov. 27	1 Chron. 23	1 Pet. 4	Mic. 2	Luke 11
Nov. 28	1 Chron. 24–25	1 Pet. 5	Mic. 3	Luke 12
Nov. 29	1 Chron. 26–27	2 Pet. 1	Mic. 4	Luke 13
Nov. 30	1 Chron. 28	2 Pet. 2	Mic. 5	Luke 14
Dec. 1	1 Chron. 29	2 Pet. 3	Mic. 6	Luke 15
Dec. 2	2 Chron. 1	1 John 1	Mic. 7	Luke 16
Dec. 3	2 Chron. 2	1 John 2	Nahum 1	Luke 17
Dec. 4	2 Chron. 3–4	1 John 3	Nah. 2	Luke 18
Dec. 5	2 Chron. 5:1–6:11	1 John 4	Nah. 3	Luke 19
Dec. 6	2 Chron. 6:12–42	1 John 5	Hab. 1	Luke 20
Dec. 7	2 Chron. 7	2 John 1	Hab. 2	Luke 21
Dec. 8	2 Chron. 8	3 John 1	Hab. 3	Luke 22
Dec. 9	2 Chron. 9	Jude 1	Zeph. 1	Luke 23
Dec. 10	2 Chron. 10	Rev. 1	Zeph. 2	Luke 24
Dec. 11	2 Chron. 11–12	Rev. 2	Zeph. 3	John 1
Dec. 12	2 Chron. 13	Rev. 3	Hag. 1	John 2
Dec. 13	2 Chron. 14–15	Rev. 4	Hag. 2	John 3
Dec. 14	2 Chron. 16	Rev. 5	Zech. 1	John 4
Dec. 15	2 Chron. 17	Rev. 6	Zech. 2	John 5
Dec. 16	2 Chron. 18	Rev. 7	Zech. 3	John 6
Dec. 17	2 Chron. 19–20	Rev. 8	Zech. 4	John 7

DATE	FAMILY		SECRET	
Dec. 18	2 Chron. 21	Rev. 9	Zech. 5	John 8
Dec. 19	2 Chron. 22-23	Rev. 10	Zech. 6	John 9
Dec. 20	2 Chron. 24	Rev. 11	Zech. 7	John 10
Dec. 21	2 Chron. 25	Rev. 12	Zech. 8	John 11
Dec. 22	2 Chron. 26	Rev. 13	Zech. 9	John 12
Dec. 23	2 Chron. 27-28	Rev. 14	Zech. 10	John 13
Dec. 24	2 Chron. 29	Rev. 15	Zech. 11	John 14
Dec. 25	2 Chron. 30	Rev. 16	Zech. 12: 1–13:1	John 15
Dec. 26	2 Chron. 31	Rev. 17	Zech. 13:2–9	John 16
Dec. 27	2 Chron. 32	Rev. 18	Zech. 14	John 17
Dec. 28	2 Chron. 33	Rev. 19	Mal. 1	John 18
Dec. 29	2 Chron. 34	Rev. 20	Mal. 2	John 19
Dec. 30	2 Chron. 35	Rev. 21	Mal. 3	John 20
Dec. 31	2 Chron. 36	Rev. 22	Mal. 4	John 21

A BASKET OF FRAMENTS

BY ROBERT MURRAY MCCHEYNE

A Sample

978-1-5271-0269-9

I
THE WORD MADE FLESH

And the Word was made flesh, and dwelt among us, (and we beheld his glory, the glory as of the only begotten of the Father) full of grace and truth (John 1:14).

You remember, brethren, when Philip went down to Samaria, it is said that he preached Christ unto them, and there was great joy in that city (Acts 8:5, 8). You remember that the apostle Paul says, 'I determined not to know anything among you, save Jesus Christ and him crucified' (1 Cor. 2:2). Now, brethren, it is really the case that the only object in the world that can give peace to your soul is 'Christ, and Him crucified'.

Those of you who are not awakened are in a great mistake in this matter; you think you have to find out something good in yourselves; you little know, dear friends, that you are seeking rest in the creature, which if you could find it, you would make out that Christ has died in vain. It is for this reason that I have chosen this text tonight, though it is so deep and full that I approach it with fear and trembling; yet certain am I that if anything will give you peace it is the getting a sight of His glory, 'the glory as of the only begotten of the Father, full of grace and truth'. It is just beholding His glory.

The first truth that is laid open here is the humiliation of the Son of God. It is laid down to us in two parts. First, 'The Word was made flesh.' Second, 'He dwelt among us.'

I. THE HUMILIATION OF THE SON OF GOD CONSISTED IN HIS BEING MADE FLESH.

I do not stop to inquire why He is called 'the Word'. I would just remark that as the word of a man expresses the mind of a man, so Christ was revealed that He might express the mind of God.

Let us consider what is meant in His being made flesh.

It is not meant that *He really took a body without a soul.* We know that Christ, as He dwelt among us, had not only a body, but a soul – a loving, human soul: 'Now is my soul troubled; and what shall I say? Father, save me from this hour: but for this cause came I unto this hour' (John 12:27)

Now, brethren, I do not so much insist upon the word 'soul', as upon 'what shall I say?' Ah, this expresses the tenderness of a human soul. Speaking with reverence, I would say, there seems to be a holy perplexity in His mind: 'Then saith he unto them, My soul is exceeding sorrowful, even unto death' (Matt. 26:38). And then the next verse shows

He had a human will: 'O my Father, if it be possible, let this cup pass from me: nevertheless not as I will, but as thou wilt.' From these passages, it is obvious that when it is said, 'The Word was made flesh', it is not meant that the Godhead was united to a human body without a soul.

Again, you are not to understand that it was a sinful body. The word 'flesh' is often used in this sense, thus: '… the flesh lusteth against the Spirit' (Gal. 5:17). Some have thought so, but it has not always this meaning; thus, in Ezekiel 36:26 it is said, 'I will take away the stony heart out of your flesh, and I will give you an heart of *flesh.*'

And, again, we know quite well from the Word of God that Christ was holy. The angels said at His birth: 'That holy thing which shall be born of thee shall be called the Son of God' (Luke 1:35). And we know that in His manhood He was holy, harmless, undefiled, and separate from sinners (Heb. 7:26). And we are expressly told that the one thing in which He differed was that He was without sin (Heb. 4:15). And we are told that in dying, 'He offered himself without spot to God' (Heb. 9:14). Now, we know that it was His human soul and body He offered up to God. So it is true that His humanity was holy.

I come now to the real meaning of the words – that He who was the second Person in the Godhead, became one with a holy human soul, and with a body with our infirmities, such as thirst, pain, capable of tears, weariness, suffering etc., for so much is implied in the word 'flesh'. 'All flesh is grass.' This is spoken of our feebleness. 'The Word was made flesh.' Great is the mystery of godliness, God was manifest in the flesh. There were three great reasons.

The first was that He might *obey the law of God in the same nature that had broken the law.* When the devil had got man to trample the law beneath His feet, as if it had never been, he thought that the law would never lift its head again. Now, the Word was made flesh that He might obey it; and so it is said, 'God sent forth his Son, made of a woman, made under the law, to redeem them that were under the law' (Gal. 4:4, 5). I remember explaining this once before to you. First, that He was made under the law that He might obey it. And then, He was made under the curse of the law that He might obey it. And then He was made under the curse of the law that He might endure it.

Now, it is to the first of these that I now speak, namely, that Christ might obey the law and do more honour to it, than if it had never been broken. This was one of the great reasons why He became flesh. If it had not been for this He might have visited the earth for an hour. But the reason why He had to stop so long was to show that it was a good law.

You know, brethren, if you look across the world, and if you take God's holy law and shed the light of it over the world, there is something overpowering to think how fearfully, His law has been broken; think of all the Sabbath-breaking there is in the world, and all the thefts, swearing, adultery, etc., all of these streaming over the world, and blotting out, as it were, the law. And oh, brethren, it is sweet to think it was worth the condescension of the Godhead becoming flesh to obey the law, so as to show to men and angels and devils that God's law was so much more honoured, than if it had never been broken.

The second reason why the Word was made flesh was *that He might die* – that He might bear the curse of the law:

> But we see Jesus, who was made a little lower than the angels for the suffering of death, crowned with glory and honour; that he by the grace of God should taste death for every man (Heb. 2:9)

> Forasmuch then as the children are partakers of flesh and blood, he also himself likewise took part of the same; that through death he might destroy him that had the power of death, that is, the devil (Heb. 2:14).

In these two verses it is distinctly said that the Word was made flesh in order that He might die. You know, brethren, if He had remained in the bosom of the Father He could not have suffered – for the divine nature cannot suffer; but in order that He might die He must be made flesh. The reason why He took upon Him a body was that He might bear the curse. You know we are under the curse; now, Christ took upon Him flesh, that He might bear the curse.

I would just mention the third reason why He was made flesh. It is *that He might have sympathy for men.*

> Wherefore in all things it behoved him to be made like unto his brethren, that he might be a merciful and faithful high priest in things pertaining to God (Heb. 2:17).

Brethren, there are no persons that can have compassion as those who have felt like us. You know God said to the Jews, You shall be kind to strangers: 'for ye know the heart of a stranger, seeing ye were strangers in the land of Egypt' (Exod. 23:9). So God says to Christ, 'You know the heart of a man.' This was one reason why He was made flesh. Those of you who are afflicted believers, you know what it is to have a friend that was tried in all points as you are.

***

To read more, visit christianfocus.com

Christian Focus Publications

Our mission statement –

STAYING FAITHFUL

In dependence upon God we seek to impact the world through literature faithful to His infallible Word, the Bible. Our aim is to ensure that the Lord Jesus Christ is presented as the only hope to obtain forgiveness of sin, live a useful life and look forward to heaven with Him.

Our books are published in four imprints:

CHRISTIAN FOCUS

Popular works including biographies, commentaries, basic doctrine and Christian living.

CHRISTIAN HERITAGE

Books representing some of the best material from the rich heritage of the church.

MENTOR

Books written at a level suitable for Bible College and seminary students, pastors, and other serious readers. The imprint includes commentaries, doctrinal studies, examination of current issues and church history.

CF4•K

Children's books for quality Bible teaching and for all age groups: Sunday school curriculum, puzzle and activity books; personal and family devotional titles, biographies and inspirational stories – because you are never too young to know Jesus!

Christian Focus Publications Ltd,
Geanies House, Fearn, Ross-shire,
IV20 1TW, Scotland, United Kingdom.
www.christianfocus.com